MW00943691

Tweets of Grace

toni kendrick

WESTBOW
PRESS®
A DIVISION OF THOMAS NELSON
& ZONDERVAN

Copyright © 2021 toni kendrick.

All rights reserved. No part of this book may be used or reproduced
by any means, graphic, electronic, or mechanical, including
photocopying, recording, taping or by any information storage
retrieval system without the written permission of the author except in
the case of brief quotations embodied in critical articles and reviews.

WestBow Press books may be ordered through
booksellers or by contacting:

WestBow Press
A Division of Thomas Nelson & Zondervan
1663 Liberty Drive
Bloomington, IN 47403
www.westbowpress.com
844-714-3454

Because of the dynamic nature of the Internet, any web
addresses or links contained in this book may have changed
since publication and may no longer be valid. The views
expressed in this work are solely those of the author and do
not necessarily reflect the views of the publisher, and the
publisher hereby disclaims any responsibility for them.

Any people depicted in stock imagery provided by Getty Images are
models, and such images are being used for illustrative purposes only.
Certain stock imagery © Getty Images.

Scripture quotations taken from The Holy Bible, New International
Version® NIV® Copyright © 1973 1978 1984 2011 by Biblica, Inc.
TM. Used by permission. All rights reserved worldwide.

Interior Image Credit: Karen McElmoyle

ISBN: 978-1-6642-3537-3 (sc)
ISBN: 978-1-6642-3538-0 (e)

Library of Congress Control Number: 2021910328

Print information available on the last page.

WestBow Press rev. date: 06/18/2021

DEDICATION

To my true friend and partner for life, Alfred.

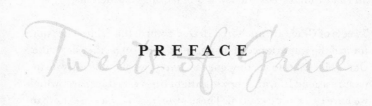

PREFACE

IN 2020, WHEN THE COVID-19 PANDEMIC BEGAN,
overwhelming feelings of fear and isolation plagued many people.
While people were concerned about catching the virus, mixed
messages from national and local officials made it difficult to
decide which advice to follow and which protection was best. Jobs
were lost, businesses failed, and many people lost loved ones.
At every level of education schools were opened, then closed,
some were conducted online, others a mixture of on-site and
online, so who knew what was best to ensure students would not
lose scholastic progress? Demonstrations and protests occurred
around the country, which sometimes became violent. People
didn't know who to trust and who to oppose. Lines were drawn
between groups with no compromise in sight.

Aside from this unusual world catastrophe, in general, I wanted
to explore how a person decides who to listen to and whose
voice is trustworthy? I wanted to find answers for the many
consequential things that come up in life; to find trustworthy
solutions I can turn to when important decisions need to be
made. I thought about words that express feelings, occurrences,
and situations that are common in life. I looked up these words in
an ancient source and then wrote brief thoughts relevant to our
contemporary circumstances. I believe the wisdom of this ancient
source is important and enduring. I call my brief thoughts,
Tweets — a term familiar to most people in our culture today. For

some, my tweets might be a reminder of how they want to tackle issues; while for others, they might be the focus of introspection and additional study – a new way of looking at problems.

Tweets of Grace are anchored in God's word, the Bible. They point toward the importance of managing our feelings; they describe God's blessings to us; they suggest habits we should cultivate to ensure a good life; and they highlight life's variables, over which we have little or no control. These offerings of grace are there to give us strength and help us make good decisions and choices so that we can have a life not marred with confusion, fear, and anger, rather, a life suffused with stability, peace, joy, and grace.

I pray that you will use these tweets to remember that God has answers, trustworthy answers, for the things we confront in life, whether we are in a pandemic, or any other situation common to life. I pray that you will find strength to tackle and overcome difficult situations and personal habits so that you can make good decisions despite the murky circumstances that may surround you. I believe there is a joyous, fulfilling life for you in the grace of Jesus Christ, and his word, the Bible, will teach you how to make the best decisions for your life.

toni kendrick

Tweets on Feelings

Why we should manage them

Feelings

anger

anxiety

compassion

fear

grief

hope

humility

jealousy

joy

lonesome

malice

pride

revenge

sadness

Your Thoughts

....

....

....

....

....

....

....

....

....

....

anger

THERE ARE A LOT OF DISAPPOINTMENTS AND inequities in this life and one response to them is to become angry. Sometimes getting angry is inevitable. Becoming angry can be a daily feeling for some people, but that feeling can rot your soul and ruin your life. Giving in to your anger and allowing it to rage prevents you from working toward a solution or a compromise to the issues that affront you. Staying angry encourages you to contemplate bad behavior and obscures your ability to rightly assess the consequences of that bad behavior. Learn to slow down, take a breath, and try to conjure up good and helpful thoughts. You can get angry but don't allow yourself to live in that place.

Everyone should be quick to listen, slow to speak and slow to become angry, for man's anger does not bring about the righteous life that God desires.

JAMES 1:19-20

Your Thoughts

....

....

....

....

....

....

....

....

....

....

....

anxiety

BEING ANXIOUS OR WORRIED DOESN'T CHANGE
anything. Being anxious and worried doesn't solve
problems, nor does it help determine solutions for our
problems. It is a feeling that causes damage. The damage
can be great, such as chronic depression, physical illness,
malicious thoughts, or scornful reactions. Avoiding
anxiety and worry should be our goal. How can you turn
anxiety into happiness? If we think our worries will be
taken care of, we release them. We relax when we know
that our concerns and 'cares' will be addressed properly
and competently. So, the lack of worry can bring the gift
of peace and happiness. That is the gift God offers us in
our relationship with him. He has pledged to take our
burdens and make them his own.

*Cast your cares (anxiety) on the Lord and he will sustain you; he will never
let the righteous fall.*

PSALMS 55:22

Your Thoughts

....

....

....

....

....

....

....

....

....

compassion

GOD HAS COMPASSION FOR US, WHETHER WE
always see it or not. The dictionary describes compassion
as *'a feeling of deep sympathy and sorrow for another who
is stricken by misfortune, accompanied by a strong desire
to alleviate the suffering'*. Compassion should be offered
not only if the misfortune that befalls a person is outside
of their control, but also, if they are somehow responsible
for their misfortune, such as exercising poor judgment or
being careless. Gratefully, when we become part of God's
'chosen people', we are made aware of God's loving care.
So, we should have compassion for others. We should see
the suffering around us and yearn to alleviate the pain,
whether we can or not.

*Therefore, as God's chosen people, holy and dearly loved, clothe yourselves
with compassion, kindness, humility, gentleness and patience. Bear
with each other and forgive whatever grievances you may have against
one another.*

COLOSSIANS 3:12-13

9

Your Thoughts

....

....

....

....

....

....

....

....

....

....

fear

THERE ARE LEVELS OF FEAR RANGING FROM
uneasiness to terror. All kinds of things can bring
a person discomfort and some things can produce
legitimate concern for safety and life. Studies have
proved that fear releases adrenaline and that activates the
body to respond. So, some 'fears' are good, but most are
not. As believers, we are taught to have no fear. We must
identify the source of our fear and recall from the bible,
'greater is He that is in us than he that is in the world'
(1 John 4:4), then move forward to face those fears. It's
okay to feel fear, but not okay to retreat into becoming an
anxious sloth who refuses to live fully because of fear.

*So do not fear, for I am with you; do not be dismayed, for I am your God.
I will strengthen you and help you; I will uphold you with my righteous
right hand. For I am the Lord, your God, who takes hold of your right
hand and says to you, Do not fear; I will help you.*
ISAIAH 41:10,13

Your Thoughts

....

....

....

....

....

....

....

....

....

....

grief

IF YOU ARE BROKENHEARTED, SOMEONE WHO
finds no pleasure in living anymore, a person whose joy
has vanished and your spirit is lost to pain and suffering,
don't despair. If the things you have had to endure are
so big and awful that you have no strength to recover,
don't despair. If you are lonely and isolated with no one
to care whether you live or die, don't despair. God cares!
He wants you to be filled with hope and joy, even if in
your current state, you don't have those things. You can
have the restoration, recovery, strength, happiness, and
comfort you need. Look to God and he will deliver you …
he promised his people that he would, and he cannot lie.

*The Lord is close to the brokenhearted and saves those who are crushed in
spirit. A righteous man may have many troubles, but the Lord delivers him
from them all.*

PSALMS 34:18–19

Your Thoughts

....

....

....

....

....

....

....

....

....

....

14

hope

"MY HOPE IS BUILT ON NOTHING LESS THAN JESUS' love and righteousness." That is the refrain of a song that always builds me up because it reminds me that hope is the birthright of a child of God. Why is it so important that hope be a birthright? Hope is energy and it is born through faith in Jesus. The energy of hope makes us strive, for our whole lives, to see the truth of God and to live in such a way that we resemble our father, Jesus Christ. That hope moves us beyond what is common, callous, or corrupt in this world and elevates our spirit and our actions to a place of splendor, excellence, and grace – it makes us better people and the world a better place.

For everything that was written in the past was written to teach us, so that through endurance and the encouragement of the Scriptures we might have hope.

ROMANS 15:4

Your Thoughts

....

....

....

....

....

....

....

....

....

humility

HUMILITY IS NOT A WORD USED REGULARLY IN our society. Rarely is the word understood, and the cultural practices on display are the opposite of humility - more like self-promotion. Why is our society so self-congratulatory? Is it because we unfairly compare ourselves to others; are we lacking self-confidence and struggling to balance that; or are we longing for recognition and reward? Most of us, if we are honest, can relate to all three of these. Think about what it means to embrace God's view of humility. A knowledge that all people have value – none superior and none inferior. Only God is to be exalted. Can we release our obsession with 'self' and contemplate that the value of another is just as important as how I value myself?

… clothe yourselves with humility toward one another, because God opposes the proud but gives grace to the humble.
1 PETER 5:5B

Your Thoughts

....

....

....

....

....

....

....

....

....

jealousy

JEALOUSY AND ENVY — THEY ARE THE SAME: wanting what does not belong to you. I call them the evil twins because some people want to make envy less offensive, so by degree, envy is slightly better than jealousy. Not so! The bible calls them both by one name — covetousness. I find that wanting something that belongs to someone else is a 'distorted' longing because you don't really know the cost of the 'thing' you covet. If you knew all that it takes to have that thing you covet, you might not even want it. So, work with what you have; enhance what you have to its most excellent form and leave other people's 'stuff' ALONE!

You shall not covet your neighbor's house. You shall not covet ... anything that belongs to your neighbor.
EXODUS 20:17

Your Thoughts

....

....

....

....

....

....

....

....

....

joy

IS THERE A DIFFERENCE BETWEEN JOY AND
happiness? Even the look of the words infers a variance —
'joy' is solidly anchored on three letters, while 'happiness'
gleefully runs along 9 letters, repeating some letters with
abandon. Happiness is a euphoric state that comes and
whips up your emotions, allows them to soar for a time,
then releases them to some other sensation. Whereas
joy is a deep-seated, solid state of being that allows you
to dwell in a secure state of substance. To enter the 'joy
of the Lord' is powerful for it allows you to have power
and might in your life. This God-given joy is not swept
away or challenged by unreliable sensations that can
ripple through you day by day, hour by hour, moment by
moment — it lingers.

> *… for the joy of the Lord is your strength.*
> NEHEMIAH 8:10B

21

Your Thoughts

....

....

....

....

....

....

....

....

....

lonesome

BEING ALONE (SEPARATE FROM OTHERS, OR
solitary) is not always an unpleasant state. Sometimes
we want or need to be alone ... to think or rest or to
accomplish something. However, being lonesome (lonely)
attaches a sad quality to the state of being alone. During
the 2020 pandemic, many people who lived alone felt
lonesome, as well as some people who live with another.
What can be done to alleviate such a state of loneliness,
depression, and solitude? Reach out! Give to someone
what you want to receive and soon you will find your
life fuller and more meaningful. The effort of caring,
supporting, offering kindness or being aware of someone
else's needs will ultimately fulfill your own.

*So in everything, do to others what you would have them do to you, for this
sums up the Law and the Prophets. (The Golden Rule)*
MATTHEW 7:12

23

Your Thoughts

....

....

....

....

....

....

....

....

....

malice

WHEN THE BIBLE TELLS ME TO 'GET RID OF'
something, then I know I have the potential to control
that thing. So too, when the bible tells me to get
something, I know that I have the capability to receive
that 'something'. Getting rid of a feeling takes a conscious
effort and it takes time. To find yourself contemplating
bad thoughts about someone or wanting some negative
outcome to visit that person is to have malice. Malice is
not reserved for evil people but can grow in the heart
of anyone. So, when you find yourself sinking into the
abyss of meanness and vengeful muses for someone –
deserving as they might be – get rid of it.

Therefore, rid yourselves of all malice and all deceit, hypocrisy, envy, and
slander of every kind. Like newborn babies, crave pure spiritual milk, so
that by it you may grow up in your salvation, now that you have tasted that
the Lord is good.

1 PETER 2:1-3

Your Thoughts

....

....

....

....

....

....

....

....

....

pride

THERE IS A DIFFERENCE BETWEEN FEELING pleasure and satisfaction over something you have accomplished or created and having an exalted opinion of yourself. One is healthy and the other is not. The idea that you are superior to others or unwilling to acquiesce your opinion or position to another (for any reason), or never feel the need to apologize for your mistakes, is an indication that you are exhibiting the 'unhealthy' pride that offends God. This feeling that allows you to indulge yourself and boast of your actions needs to be controlled and extinguished. It will only destroy you in the end. It is a character flaw with dramatic results – enough said!

The Lord detests all the proud of heart. Be sure of this: They will not go unpunished.

PROVERBS 16:5

Your Thoughts

....

....

....

....

....

....

....

....

....

revenge

WHEN I THINK OF REVENGE, I THINK OF
something big – a big payback for a big injustice or insult.
I mustn't forget that life consists of lots of injustices and
insults and often we get caught up in retaliating. Also,
we blow up the offenses we perceive to be larger than
they might have been, initially. You know, the driver who
cuts you off, so you speed up to return the same. Or the
sarcastic retort which you match to another's sarcastic
comment. We forget that we don't have to respond to every
slight we perceive. The idea of letting go of an offense is
foreign to some of us and we would do well to learn that
true vengeance is in the province of God.

*Do not repay evil with evil or insult with insult, but with blessing, because
to this you were called so that you may inherit a blessing.*
1 PETER 3:9

Your Thoughts

....

....

....

....

....

....

....

....

sadness

DEPRESSION IS WIDESPREAD IN OUR SOCIETY. IT is not a brief sadness, but a condition of being debilitated. The dictionary says this condition is *"more prolonged than that warranted by any objective reason."* How does a creation of the God of hope and might come to be destroyed by an apathy that feels too big to overcome? God does not want us to live in a state of hopelessness and he provides a way for us to clear ourselves of this misery. God's word, the Bible, has answers. If you believe in God, you can find the strength you need to fight the tentacles of despair that threaten your life and drain your energy. Trust in the Lord; search his word, you will find help.

But you are a chosen people, a royal priesthood, a holy nation, a people belonging to God, that you may declare the praises of him who called you out of darkness into his wonderful light.

1 PETER 2:9

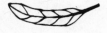

Tweets on Blessings

God's gifts to us

Blessings

abundance

choices

courage

friendship

good thoughts

instructions

nature

peace

second chances

sleep

strength

talents

twosome

wisdom

the word

Give Thanks!

....

....

....

....

....

....

....

....

....

....

abundance

ABUNDANCE IN CHRIST IS NOT 'STUFF'.
Abundance in Christ are intrinsic things that allow a
person to excel in talent and compassion, to serve with
wisdom and might, and to add to the advancement of
mankind. God is always interested in the big picture: not
making sure we have the most beautiful clothes, jewelry,
homes, vacations ... you know, the stuff we preoccupy
ourselves with most days. Being rich is not an abundance
of assets, although having riches is not precluded. Jesus
said, "Watch out! Be on your guard against all kinds of
greed; a man's life does not consist in the abundance of
his possessions." (Luke 12:15) But since God promised
abundance, find out exactly what that means ... it's
different from the 'stuff' of our culture.

If you fully obey the Lord your God and carefully follow all his commands,
I give you today, the Lord your God will set you high above all the nations
on earth. The Lord will grant you abundant prosperity ...
DEUTERONOMY 28:1, 11

Give Thanks!

....

....

....

....

....

....

....

....

....

....

....

....

choices

WE HAVE CHOICES ... THAT IS WHAT MY MOTHER
always told me. We were made by God, in his image,
which is a 'freedom' he gave to all mankind. That freedom
includes choosing to believe in him, or not. In a free
society, we can make many choices, from what to eat, how
to dress, where to live and how to behave. For those of us
who believe in God, our choices must be anchored by our
faith – a belief in things we hope for but do not always
see or have. It is that choice to believe in a good God that
compels us to be good, compassionate, helpful, just, and
principled people, even when it seems futile. It is that
faith that gives our choices character and makes them
sound.

*Faith by itself, if it is not accompanied by action is dead. Also, As the body
without the spirit is dead, so faith without deeds is dead.*
JAMES 2:17, 26

Give Thanks!

....

....

....

....

....

....

....

....

....

courage

BEING BRAVE, STANDING FIRM, FACING DIFFICULTY
… all these describe a character that masters fear and has
a purpose. In life, we are born or thrust into situations
that do not foster the kind of character that is courageous.
God sent his son, Jesus Christ, to rescue us from that fate.
We do not have to be defined by our 'history'. We do not
have to have attitudes that are dispirited, biased, cruel, or
fearful. We can have the abundant life gifted to us by Jesus
Christ. Do you have the courage to face, and then stand
firm against your history, and fight the hardships before
you? If you use the strength of Christ to find the courage
you need, you can face every obstacle in your path.

*Be strong and very courageous. Be careful to obey all the law my servant
Moses gave you; to not turn from it to the right or to the left, that you may
be successful wherever you go. … Be strong and courageous. Do not be
terrified; do not be discouraged, for the Lord your God will be with you
wherever you go.*

JOSHUA 1:7 & 9

Give Thanks!

....

....

....

....

....

....

....

....

....

....

....

friendship

I HAVE SOMETIMES CONFUSED A GOOD 'COMRADE' with a true 'friend'. Someone with whom I work, or share an activity, or an interest, I might have thought of as a 'friend', but over the years I have learned that often they were instead, a comrade. When the strands of our connection have ended, a comrade often will disappear from my life. At those moments, I have wondered what happened to my friend. The idea of a friend, much like the word "love", has been misused and misunderstood in our contemporary society. A friend is so much more than someone to hang out with, so much more than having someone always agree with us. A friend is a trusted ally that has depth, endurance, caring, sanctuary, and sometimes, gives critique. It is another of God's great gifts to humanity.

A friend loves at all times ..., also, Wounds of a friend can be trusted, ...
PROVERBS 17:17 & 27:6

43

Give Thanks!

....

....

....

....

....

....

....

....

....

good thoughts

THE BIBLE IN PROVERBS 4:23 SAYS WE MUST,
"guard our heart" — I love to recall that. It reminds me
that my thoughts and what I love are mine to treasure and
protect. Jesus said, "Out of the overflow of the heart the
mouth speaks," (Matthew 12:33) and "By their fruit you
will recognize them" (Matthew 7:16). These scriptures are
signposts to me that I must control my thoughts because
they are the bedrock of my soul. So, what I think about,
how I process my experiences, what I choose to embrace
and believe will be apparent by how I speak and how I live.
You can't hide your true self. Who you are will eventually
be revealed, so, choose to work diligently at having good
stuff inside, so that good stuff will flow out of you.

*Finally brothers, whatever is true, whatever is noble, whatever is pure,
whatever is lovely, whatever is admirable — if anything is excellent or
praiseworthy — think about such things.*

PHILIPPIANS 4:8

Give Thanks!

....

....

....

....

....

....

....

....

....

instructions

WHY SHOULD WE, AS CHRISTIANS, READ THE bible and follow God's commands? The best answer to that question was answered by Jesus, as well as a great 'cloud' of witnesses who have testified to the value of following God's instructions for living. It is explained, most expertly in Psalms 19:7-9, 11: "The law of the Lord is perfect, reviving the soul. The statutes of the Lord are trustworthy, making wise the simple. The precepts of the Lord are right, giving joy to the heart. The commands of the Lord are radiant, giving light to the eyes. The fear of the Lord is pure, enduring forever. The ordinances of the Lord are sure and altogether righteous. By them is your servant warned; in keeping them there is great reward."

Jesus said, I am the light of the world. Whoever follows me will never walk in darkness but will have the light of life. If you hold to my teaching, you are really my disciples. Then you will know the truth, and the truth will set you free.

JOHN 8:12, 31-32

Give Thanks!

....

....

....

....

....

....

....

....

....

nature

NATURE IS A MAJESTIC, MESMERIZING, DELIGHTFUL, inspiring, fearsome thing. No one is taught to experience emotions when gazing at the high, low, wet, dry, icy, floral, wooded, arid, sandy, rocky, or lush places on this earth. Our emotions surface, unbidden, and we are humbled, awed, and intrigued by the wonder of nature. We feel awe as we witness the intricacies of various animals, fish, and fowl and they stir us in mighty ways. God says he created these things to give us evidence of him and his might. Our reaction to them should lead us to him and, yet we still seek to find proof that God exists. I say, behold the obvious and be blessed … all who are willing to see.

The God who made the world and everything in it is the Lord of heaven and earth … God did this so that men would seek him and perhaps reach out for him and find him …
ACTS 17:24, 27

Give Thanks!

....

....

....

....

....

....

....

....

....

peace

WHEN CHAOS AND DANGER SWIRL ALL AROUND
you, are you crouched in fear and trembling, waiting for
disaster to overtake you? No doubt, in such a situation,
you are alarmed and fearful, but God has given us a
promise that we need not become disabled by fear. He
has bestowed on his loved ones the ability to 'don' a
peace that is inexplicable. That peace comes from the
knowledge that God is our rock and shield. He will not
allow anything to befall us that we cannot 'bear' and he
will be with us through everything we encounter. Master
your fear and live peacefully … because you can!

*…by prayer and petition, with thanksgiving, present your requests to God.
And the peace of God, which transcends all understanding, will guard your
hearts and your minds in Christ Jesus.*
PHILIPPIANS 4:5B–6

Give Thanks!

....

....

....

....

....

....

....

....

....

second chances

SOMETIMES WE WISH WE COULD GO BACK AND have a second chance to do something … what we refer to these days as 'do over'. Perhaps, we would have a better outcome if we could change how we responded to something. Suddenly, we understand that our choice has landed us in a place that is not optimal, and we recognize another choice would have (might have) offered a better outcome. God knew that we would make some wrong choices and he sent help for our situation thousands of years ago. He gave us a 'second chance' at living our best life. He 'redeemed' us with the love and sacrifice of Jesus Christ, his son. So, now with this second chance, will we once again make the wrong decision, or will we choose rightly this time?

I will give you a new heart and put a new spirit in you; I will remove from you your heart of stone and give you a heart of flesh. And I will put my Spirit in you and move you to follow my decrees and be careful to keep my laws.

EZEKIEL 36:26–27

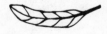

Give Thanks!

....

....

....

....

....

....

....

....

....

....

sleep

EACH MORNING, DEAR LORD, WHEN I OPEN MY
eyes and my mind flows back into place, I am grateful for
a night of restorative, peaceful sleep. You alone provide
the lift I feel in my body and spirit as I arise to the
clemency of your noble grace. If I awake and feel heavy
and tired, I know there is another, more recuperative
sleep I can possess. So, when I lie down at night, not
always alert to the land of chance I am entering, I am
humbled by the safe passage you afford me and the peace
that can be mine as I slumber. My nightly prayer should
always be, Lord grant me the rest and renewal that comes
from your grace.

*I will lie down and sleep in peace, for you alone, O Lord, make me dwell
in safety.*

PSALMS 4:8

Give Thanks!

....

....

....

....

....

....

....

....

....

strength

AM I STRONG? I THINK SO. I KNOW I LIKE THE
idea of being strong. No one is strong all the time or in
all things, but in general, I try to be strong. I don't aim
for physical strength only, although I want a measure
of that. What I want is emotional, intellectual, and
spiritual strength. The real challenge is to be strong
when it counts the most. To stand firm when survival and
character are at risk, knowing that being weak will have
outcomes I don't want to experience. The key to my being
strong is receiving God's strength. With His power I gain
discipline to control my emotions, and wisdom to inform
my decisions and choices.

*The Lord is my strength and my shield; my heart trusts in him and I am
helped. The Lord is the strength of his people.*
PSALMS 28:4A, 5

Give Thanks!

....

....

....

....

....

....

....

....

....

talents

OUR TALENTS, OR GIFTS, OR CREATIVITY
(whichever word suits you) are given to us by God.
Understanding that we all have talent is important
because it should allow us to celebrate and benefit from
the talents of others; not be envious of them. In addition,
we should have a sense of our value in the world because
we, too, have some special talent to offer. Our challenge,
sometimes, is to identify what are our talents. Good
parents help with that; but if you don't get that parental
astuteness, pay attention to what comes most easily to
you and soon you will discover your natural, God-given
ability – then work with it. God gave it to you to 'brighten
the corner' wherever you are … so do it!

*Every good and perfect gift is from above, coming down from the Father of
the heavenly lights, who does not change like shifting shadows.*
JAMES 1:17

Give Thanks!

....

....

....

....

....

....

....

....

....

....

....

....

twosome

THE BIBLE'S MENTION OF A 'TWOSOME' MAY
require some interpretation. These days there are many
kinds of partnerships. Without me defining that, I trust
any duo that operates agreeably is beneficial. It can be
spouses, parent-child, friends, siblings, whatever - the
point is, being in a trusted relationship is favorable to
one's life. I believe that and have benefitted for many
decades from being part of a couple. So here is the secret
to successful coupling —a 'twosome' takes continuous
effort and unwavering commitment, no shortcuts, no
intermissions. God's advice is, don't go it alone, there is
great reward for the work in being a twosome.

*Two are better than one because they have a good return for their work:
If one falls down, his friend can help him up. ...Also, if two lay down
together, they will keep warm. But how can one keep warm alone?
Though one may be overpowered, two can defend themselves.*

ECCLESIASTES 4:9-12

61

Give Thanks!

....

....

....

....

....

....

....

....

....

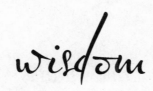

wisdom

IN OUR SOCIETY, WISDOM IS NOT SOMETHING
people talk about very much. I don't hear many people
describing someone else as 'wise'. People don't include
that attribute as part of their decision-making, such as,
"It was the wise thing to do." Many young people look
to their friends for advice, rather than an older, more
experienced person. Sadly, the quest to learn answers
to the conundrums we face in our lives doesn't always
include wisdom as part of that search. I believe that
God uses our experiences (and others') to enlighten us
to solutions and pitfalls, and this knowledge is there to
help us do better ... as well as to teach others what we've
learned. Wisdom is God's gift to us for a good life!

*Do not forsake wisdom, and she will protect you; love her, and she will
watch over you. Wisdom is supreme; therefore, get wisdom. Though it cost
all you have, get understanding.*
PROVERBS 4:6–7

Give Thanks!

....

....

....

....

....

....

....

....

....

the word

GOD'S WORD IS POWERFUL! CAN YOU HEAR THAT?
Do you really understand what that means? God's word,
the Bible, contains life and all the understanding one
needs to live, and to live gloriously. The more you read
and comprehend the words of life that God has given
to us, the more valuable and meaningful your life will
be. You will not suffer the confusion and sorrow a life
void of God will suffer. The Bible says the word is 'living
and active' because nothing is 'hidden from God's
sight'. When you speak God's word, you bring power and
resolution to your circumstances. So, look to the master,
to the creator, to the Lord for help and understanding,
and then receive the grace, mercy, peace, power, and joy
that only come from him. Ahhhhh!

*... so is my word that goes out from my mouth; it will not return to me
empty but will accomplish what I desire and achieve the purpose for which
I sent it.*

ISAIAH 55:11

Tweets on Habits

Ones we should cultivate

Habits

behavior
believe
celebration
change
discernment
forgive
give love
kindness
obedience
order
patience
praise
prayer
repentance
self-control
service
thankful
tell the truth

Needs work...

....

....

....

....

....

....

....

....

....

behavior

IS THERE A 'GOOD' BEHAVIOR AND A 'BAD' behavior? If so, why is it important to label actions as 'good' or 'bad'? Perhaps, because behavior has a consequence, and those consequences can be beneficial or detrimental to the person demonstrating the behavior. It is the 'consequence' that determines if the behavior is good or bad. The real question is how to distinguish which behavior will have which outcome. We have help with that and it is in the Bible. The word of God tells us, which is which, and if you want to ensure your life has the best consequences when you ease down the road of life, behave decently ... the Bible tells you how!

Let us behave decently, as in the daytime, not in orgies and drunkenness, not in sexual immorality and debauchery, not in dissension and jealousy. Rather, clothe yourselves with the Lord Jesus Christ.

ROMANS 13:13

Needs work...

....

....

....

....

....

....

....

....

....

believe

MY HUSBAND TOLD ME ONCE THAT IF ANY MAN can do something then so can he. At that moment, I wasn't so sure if I believed that. However, upon reflection, I realized that he meant the human mind and body has universal potential and if one can determine something for himself/herself, then they can achieve it. So, yes, I now understand that what we believe of ourselves is the first step to achieving something, anything, everything. This also means our actions and resolves must follow our beliefs. Passion, commitment, tenacity, and regard are signs of true belief, which is the secret to success.

Jesus said, Everything is possible for him who believes.
MARK 9:23

Needs work...

....

....

....

....

....

....

....

....

....

celebration

KING SOLOMON IS KNOWN FOR HIS MIGHT AND
wisdom. In the bible, he shared his knowledge about
things he observed and learned from his mighty position
as a King and as a man of God. Ultimately, he advised man
to live joyfully and to fully experience this life because
it is given to us by God. Even the Apostle Paul (1 Cor.
10:26, 31), many years after King Solomon, advised God's
followers that, "*The earth is the Lord's, and everything in
it. … So, whether you eat or drink or whatever you do, do it
all for the glory of God.*" It is uplifting to understand that
when we have an opportunity to partake in any of God's
blessings (no matter what is going on in the world), it is
okay for us to enjoy them.

*I know that there is nothing better for men than to be happy and do good
while they live. That everyone may eat and drink and find satisfaction in
all his toil — this is the gift of God.*
ECCLESIASTES 3:12–13

Needs work...

....

....

....

....

....

....

....

....

....

change

IN OUR RAPIDLY CHANGING WORLD, DEMANDS TO
be flexible and creative abound. As individuals, sometimes
the need to move things around creeps in and changes
our resolve and we become the agent of change. But what
should we do about the ever-shifting norms in society?
Should our response to changes we initiate differ from
those changes that are thrust upon us by others? I believe
we should adhere to those paradigms that form the basis
of our core beliefs, and then 'bend'. It is necessary to
embrace transitions, shifts, adjustments, modifications,
and transformations that enable us to grow and advance.
But we should maintain our core beliefs, and for me,
that means I must always keep God's commands despite
societal norms. That is the best way for me to face change.

*But the plans of the Lord stand firm forever, the purposes of his heart
through all generations.*

PSALMS 33:11

Needs work...

....

....

....

....

....

....

....

....

....

....

discernment

IT IS IMPORTANT TO KNOW THE DIFFERENCE
between judging someone and 'discerning' personally
what is right and wrong, or good and bad. Only God
can pass judgment on a person because he alone knows
everything involved in a person's life. Only a 'just'
God will determine who receives punishment and who
receives reward. But each of us needs to examine the
things in our life to recognize what is good and right
according to our moral standards. We should not resent
another person's decision that differs from ours, nor
do we have to relinquish our standards to appear non-
judgmental. We can differ, with kindness, because we
each have the right to choose what we want to accept and
reject. I just pray my decisions are based on God's laws
and not man's.

And this is my prayer: that your love may abound more and more in
knowledge and depth of insight, so that you may be able to discern
what is best ...

PHILIPPIANS 1:9–10

Needs work...

....

....

....

....

....

....

....

....

....

forgive

IT TOOK ME A LONG TIME AND A LOT OF BIBLE
study to understand what it means to be truly forgiving.
I don't mean just saying the words, I forgive, but
understanding what it really means to forgive someone.
It took me some time to understand, not because I was
unwilling to forgive, but some acts against another are so
horrific and devastating that I could not understand how
those acts (intentional acts, especially) could be forgiven.
Forgiveness is the act of releasing feelings of anger,
hatred, vengeance, and bitterness from your mind and
ultimately from your emotions. It doesn't mean a restored
relationship with the offender or adopting amnesia
about the event. It means you release all retaliation of
the offence to God, the perfect judge. Thus, practicing
forgiveness is a habit you can develop; it is a 'healthy
choice'; one that allows your pain to eventually dissipate.

Bear with each other and forgive whatever grievances you may have
against one another. Forgive as the Lord forgave you.
COLOSSIANS 3:13

Needs work...

....

....

....

....

....

....

....

....

....

....

give love

THERE ARE SEVERAL DEFINITIONS THAT DESCRIBE love. From the ancient Greeks, we learned there is, selfless unconditional love (agape); sexual attraction (eros); affectionate love to others (philia); care of family and friends (storge), childish playful love (ludus); long-term, enduring love between partners (pragma); and love of oneself (philautia). All these types of love aptly describe to whom and when we can show love. So, what does God expect of us when he asks us to 'give love'. The definition of giving is: *"to present voluntarily and without expecting compensation."* When God tells us to give love, it covers all the various ways we can show concern and care for others. If we want to know the fulsome of God's love, then we must give love, every kind of love, for our entire life.

...let us love one another, for love comes from God. Everyone who loves has been born of God and knows God. Whoever does not love does not know God, because God is love.

1 JOHN 4:7

Needs work...

....

....

....

....

....

....

....

....

....

....

kindness

BEING KIND IS A DISPOSITION OR DEMEANOR WE
can choose to assume. True kindness is not edged with
sarcasm or irritation, and it takes effort to practice being
kind. Some people have worked toward adopting this
disposition early on, so that it seems effortless as the
years go by. But some people are still working toward
that goal. Throughout the bible, God has commanded his
followers to adopt this disposition as a character trait. We
don't get to ignore this command; we must offer gentle,
patient, thoughtful, considerate, helpful, sympathetic
interactions with others. Being kind is who we need to be!

*Make sure that nobody pays back wrong for wrong, but always try to be
kind to each other and to everyone else.*
1 THESSALONIANS 5:15

Needs work...

....

....

....

....

....

....

....

....

obedience

IS OBEDIENCE THE KEY OR A KEY ... KEY TO
what? One of the first lessons a responsible parent tries to
teach their child is obedience. It is through the child's act
of submission that a parent can protect and guide them. If
a child does not learn, in the early years, to submit to the
authority of their parents, then most likely they will often
defy all authority and seek to live by their own dictates.
Pride is the root of disobedience – a refusal to submit
because we think we know best. So why is obedience so
important in the life of a Christian? Because God offers
guidance to protect us and give us the life **he** designed for
us, and because it shows respect and trust. Greater still,
obedience to his instructions will save our lives.

*Take to heart to all the words I have solemnly declared to you this day, so
that you may command your children to obey carefully all the words of this
law. They are not just idle words for you – they are your life.*
DEUTERONOMY 32:46–47

87

Needs work...

....

....

....

....

....

....

....

....

....

....

order

WHEN I WAS A SMALL GIRL, MY NANA TOLD ME,
"God is not the author of confusion but of peace." She
may have said it more than once, but eventually I was
impressed with the notion that to be orderly was a good
thing. Later she told me, "If you give everything in your
house a 'home', you will never lose anything." Again,
sage advice from a woman of God. How useful that one
concept has been in my life. It doesn't mean that disorder,
confusion, disarray, or discord should never enter your
life. It does mean they should not become a way of life.
Life can be messy, but striving for order, tidiness, and
harmony is a God-given directive that brings the kind of
life God intended us to live.

For God is not a God of disorder but of peace.
1 CORINTHIANS 14:33

Needs work...

....

....

....

....

....

....

....

....

....

....

patience

BEING PATIENT IS NOT JUST THE ABILITY TO
quietly wait for something or calmly endure something,
but that 'waiting' must be without complaint, annoyance,
loss of temper, or anything etched with irritation.
Developing patience is an arduous discipline, especially
for some people. Training oneself to persevere, delay,
endure or be diligent without complaint, annoyance, loss
of temper or irritation is important for building character.
So, what is the basis for gaining patience? LOVE! Recall a
loving parent trying to help their young child understand
something, or accept something, or even eat something.
They tenderly and kindly keep nudging that child toward
something beneficial. That is how God nudges us toward a
good character and a good life – with patience.

Love is patient, love is kind. It does not envy, it does not boast, it is not proud.
It is not rude, it is not self-seeking, it is not easily angered, it keeps no record
of wrongs. Love does not delight in evil but rejoices with the truth. It always
protects, always trusts, always hopes, always perseveres. Love never fails.
1 CORINTHIANS 13:4–8

Needs work…

....

....

....

....

....

....

....

....

....

praise

THE ACT OF MENTIONING SOMETHING WONDERFUL
is not foreign to anyone. All people enjoy being
commended for good deeds, excellence, thoughtfulness,
talent, sacrifice, etc. But most especially, when
something is above ordinary and undeserved (such as
God's grace), the expressions of admiration for those
extraordinary acts/events are (should be) enormous. A
God that designed such a magnificent world, created such
miraculous beings, and loves in such incomprehensible
ways deserves mention, and that 'mention' is praise.
How can we acknowledge our understanding of and
appreciation for his unfathomable gifts? By praising him,
day and night, in every situation — we should praise him!

Let everything that has breath praise the Lord. Praise the Lord.
PSALMS 150:6

Needs work...

....

....

....

....

....

....

....

....

....

prayer

WHEN YOU PRAY, YOU OPEN YOUR SOUL. YOU
find connection with your inner desires or fears and you
offer them up for celebration or help. The act of quieting
oneself and searching within … for what is missing,
what is needed, what is joyous, what is scared, what is
hopeful … brings healing and tranquility. The privacy
of this connection is matchless. Revealing some private
or vulnerable part of yourself to a friend or a partner can
be risky, and some risks are too consequential to chance.
But prayer, to a benevolent God, is just what is needed to
empty your heart and find a safe harbor to anchor your
private, vulnerable parts. Try it, it works!

*Jesus said, Therefore, I tell you, whatever you ask for in prayer, believe that
you have received it, and it will be yours.*
MARK 11:24

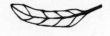

Needs work...

....

....

....

....

....

....

....

....

....

repentance

GOD MADE US, SO HE KNOWS OUR FLAWS AND
weaknesses. Our flaws and weaknesses separate us from
him. Therefore, God made the ultimate 'reparation'
(renewal/forgiveness) for us through Jesus Christ.
To receive this reparation, we must repent for our
shortcomings. Repenting is different from an apology.
An apology can be offered to be socially correct, or
to defuse a situation. But true repentance involves
regret and a desire for a change in action, attitude, or
conviction. There is no forgiveness without repentance.
The same is true in our relationship with others: genuine
repentance must be offered to restore brokenness. True
repentance begets true forgiveness.

*Godly sorrow brings repentance that leads to salvation and leaves no
regret, but worldly sorrow brings death.*
2 CORINTHIANS 7:10

Needs work...

....

....

....

....

....

....

....

....

....

self-control

SELF-CONTROL, LIKE EXERCISING FAITH, IS
fueled by certain things: trust, commitment, patience,
love, and obedience. The bible cautions us to exercise
self-control in many scriptures and in many situations.
But why self-control? Because the lack of it leads to
sin. Having self-control means taking care with how
we respond and how we behave. Taking time to reflect
on the consequences and effects of our actions. Taking
time to consider another perspective that might help us
better understand a situation or our response to it. There
are rewards for having self-control, such as, success
in realizing outcomes, and greatest of all, receiving
blessings from a loving and just God – that's the biggest
reward of all.

*But since we belong to the day, let us be self-controlled, putting on faith
and love as a breastplate, and the hope of salvation as a helmet.*
1 THESSALONIANS 5:8

Needs work...

....

....

....

....

....

....

....

....

....

service

BEING USEFUL GIVES A PERSON PURPOSE.
Performing a task allows one to gain knowledge and
skill. Helping others creates feelings of compassion and
empathy. It helps a person understand another. This
is one of the great benefits of serving. Another benefit
of serving is that you offer your talents and skills to
the world and thus fulfill God's purpose for your life.
Every person should find time and opportunity to
serve someone else. That service can be in a family, a
community, a job, an assignment, anything where you
offer up yourself to an endeavor where someone else gets
help ... your benefit comes later, after you serve.

... whoever wants to become great among you must be your servant, and
whoever wants to be first must be your slave — just as the Son of Man did
not come to be served, but to serve.

MATTHEWS 20:26-28

Needs work...

....

....

....

....

....

....

....

....

....

....

thankful

WHEN EVERYTHING IS GOING WELL WITH YOU,
give thanks. When things are not going well, give thanks.
If you are in an uncomfortable or desperate situation
and don't have a solution, give thanks. If you are sick or
injured and your body is unable to function properly,
still give thanks. If your life is brimming with blessings,
instead of feeling unworthy, just give thanks. When you
fail and all your efforts 'misfire', insist on giving thanks.
Giving thanks means finding something positive in your
life and telling God, THANK YOU. Giving thanks means
taking a moment to recall that bad situations come and
go, and good times come around again. Giving thanks
means releasing outcomes to the Lord Jesus Christ,
knowing that he is the solution that never fails. So, just
give thanks ... always.

...give thanks in all circumstances, for this is God's will for you in
Christ Jesus.

1 THESSALONIANS 5:18

Needs work...

....

....

....

....

....

....

....

....

....

tell the truth

AS A CHRISTIAN, I LEARNED THAT BEING
truthful is a God-given command. Telling the truth is
important and I think we all know that. We often defend
what we call 'white' lies, believing they are innocent and
sometimes kinder than telling the truth. But, in fact,
we are inundated with the selfish manipulation of facts.
Nevertheless, God wants us to tell the truth. He wants
us to live authentically and to be genuine in every way,
including what we say and what we 'own' up to. Are you
willing to allow truthfulness to begin in you – in your
heart, words, and actions. I say, tell the truth. It is the
beginning of true freedom and peace.

*They perish because they refused to love the truth and to be saved. For this
reason, God sends them a powerful delusion so that they will believe the lie
and so that all will be condemned who have not believed the truth but have
delighted in (lies).*
2 THESSALONIANS 2: 10-12

105

Tweets on Life

Variables we don't control

Life

death

enemy

justice

life

getting older

seasons

trials

being a woman

work

youth

I get it!

....

....

....

....

....

....

....

....

....

death

WHEN I THINK OF DEATH (NOT NECESSARILY MY own), and particularly the loss of someone I love, what am I to do? How do I comfort another who is facing life without a loved one? The loss, the emptiness, the cancellation of hopes and dreams with another are real and somehow, must be resolved. Even when tragedy or sudden death descends on someone, how do we find peace with the abruptness of that loss. I believe, we are not to grieve like those who have no hope, because as a child of God, we have been given hope, peace, and strength that will allow us to endure. Those comforts are in the hands of God and he will give them to us — we must learn to lean into him.

... for death is the destiny of every man; the living should take this to heart.
ECCLESIASTES 7:2B

I get it!

enemy

IT IS UNCOMFORTABLE TO KNOW THAT SOMEONE is out to get you - to know, someone has a mission to destroy you. It is more than uncomfortable; it is downright frightening. But to be warned allows you to protect yourself; to be ready for and armed against the attack. What is essential is to have sufficient 'armor' to fight the imminent assault. God has alerted us that we are under attack, and he has also equipped us with what is needed to disable the onslaught. He says, "Put on the full armor of God so that you can take your stand against the devil's schemes." (Eph. 6:11) Praise God we don't have to be surprised. All we need to do is use his armor and win the war!

Be self-controlled and alert. Your enemy the devil prowls around like a roaring lion looking for someone to devour. Resist him ...
1 PETER 1:8-9A

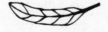

I get it!

....

....

....

....

....

....

....

....

....

....

justice

EVERYONE WANTS TO RECEIVE JUSTICE, BUT HOW
many of us extend justice? We live in a time when we
can hear and see injustices everywhere in the world. We
don't always get the full story behind every perceived
injustice, but some things are so wrong that you don't
need a backstory to know that the cruelty, suffering, and
damage you see is a result of an imbalance. We should
always choose to be just. We must stand against inequity
because it is wrong. God says, "Do not follow the crowd in
doing wrong. When you give testimony in a lawsuit, do not
pervert justice by siding with the crowd, and do not show
favoritism to a poor man in his lawsuit." (Exodus 28:2) Do
we get it? God wants justice to prevail, for everyone, always.

*Evil men do not understand justice, but those who seek the Lord
understand it fully.*

PROVERBS 28:5

I get it!

....

....

....

....

....

....

....

....

....

life

THE ITALIANS HAVE A SAYING THAT THEY UTTER when they can't explain life's good or bad moments. They say, "è la vita!" (It's the life) and it mollifies them because there is no further explanation. This great journey of life is inexplicable; things happen that can change the pattern of a life in a good or bad direction. There is no easy answer to every conundrum nor is there justice for every injury. There are some discernible patterns to follow, but the greatest assurance of purpose for our lives comes from God, and it is given to his followers. He offers a future where there are answers, and justice, and order, and peace. So, listen up (the sooner the better), follow Christ and seize a life that makes sense and is filled with his grace.

Blessed is the man who listens to me, watching daily at my doors, waiting at my doorway. For whoever finds me finds life and receives favor from the Lord.

PROVERBS 8:34–35

I get it!

....

....

....

....

....

....

....

....

....

getting older

WHAT IS THE DIFFERENCE BETWEEN BEING OLD and being older? Maybe for some younger folks, everyone over a certain age is just 'old'. As I age, I think of myself as 'older' and that moniker is kinder and less limiting than the word, old. Our society tries to 'handle' older folk in a particular way, often unpleasantly. They don't see the same diversities in older folk that they see in younger folk, nor do they pay attention to the life experiences of older folk. There are a plethora of talents and skills that distinguishes each of us. So why, when folks are over 60, are they viewed as homogeneous and expected to remove themselves to the edges of society to quietly wait for death? Being older has its pitfalls, but drabness and solitude should not be the destiny of older folks. God promised to be with us until the end, so he expects us to stay in the fray of life and contribute until we are no more.

Even to your old age and gray hairs I am he, I am he who will sustain you. I have made you and I will carry you; I will sustain you and I will rescue you.
ISAIAH 46:4

I get it!

Seasons

AT THIS EPOCH IN HISTORY (APRIL OF 2020), there is a pandemic (COVID-19) that has infected multimillions of people in the world and has also killed millions. Watching what is changing in the United States, in my state of North Carolina, and in my city of Charlotte, shows me that habits and practices will change because this 'season of illness' has affected every facet of our lives. But we, believers in Christ, are to remain hopeful and energized because this, too, is under God's watchful eye. He will sustain us and give us what we need to change and adapt to whatever we must in this life. In the bible, Psalms 31:15 says, "My times are in your (God's) hands", and they are. We must have faith that we will emerge from each season we live through ... and be saved.

There is a time for everything, and a season for every activity under heaven.
ECCLESIASTES 3:1

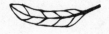

I get it!

....

....

....

....

....

....

....

....

....

....

trials

WHAT IS THE DIFFERENCE BETWEEN A TRIAL AND
a temptation? Understanding the distinction between
the two is important in our quest to manage both. Trials
are things that happen to us that can pose a challenge to
our faith. Being tempted to respond to these challenges
with sinful practices, behaviors, feelings, or habits, is not
the response God intends. God will send and allow us to
have trials, but the purpose of his trials is not to lure us
to sinfulness. God wants us to conquer problems so that
we can mature as Christians. We are expected to endure
hardships, as a training to increase our faith. God never
will try to defeat us by tempting us toward sinful practices
or habits. Those are the tools of our enemy, the devil.
Remember, God is always with us, and he gives us what we
need to be victorious in our challenges!

*No temptation has seized you except what is common to man. And God is
faithful; he will not let you be tempted beyond what you can bear. But when you
are tempted, he will also provide a way out so that you can stand up under it.*
1 CORINTHIANS 10:13

123

I get it!

....

....

....

....

....

....

....

....

....

....

being a woman

THERE IS SO MUCH DISCUSSION, SO MUCH ANGST, so much variance about what it means to be a woman, and her place in this world. The design of woman is like that of a man, for she was made from the same pattern. The role, intent, function of her existence was to be a twosome with man, and it was deemed suitable — not inferior. Why is that so difficult? The purpose of her life is to have a good character, be responsible, add value to the world, and honor God - it is the same for all God's creations. It was never intended for a woman to be the 'property' of a man. A woman is given life to live freely and to exercise her God-given talents — same as a man.

The Lord God said, 'It is not good for the man to be alone. I will make a helper suitable for him.' Then the Lord God made a woman from the rib he had taken out of the man, and he brought her to the man.

GENESIS 2:18, 22

125

I get it!

....

....

....

....

....

....

....

....

....

OUR WORK DEFINES US. IT DOESN'T MATTER
what 'work' we do; it demonstrates our integrity,
strength, commitment, talent, and discipline ... or lack
thereof. To bring good quality to our work, we must have
a driving force, a passion to ignite our energy so that we
can attend to our work in a excellent way. Some jobs may
seem as if they are of lesser significance, but everything
we do is our work for that moment and deserves our total
attention. Additionally, we must understand that all
work includes toil, difficulty, lack of acknowledgement,
sacrifice, and maybe tedium at times, but our commitment to work must never waiver. Remember, our work
reflects our character and is, therefore, our legacy.

*Whatever you do, work at it with all your heart, as working for the Lord,
not for men, since you know that you will receive an inheritance from the
Lord as a reward. It is the Lord Christ you are serving.*
COLOSSIANS 3:23-24

I get it!

....

....

....

....

....

....

....

....

....

....

youth

IT IS A HUGE ADVANTAGE TO BE INTRODUCED TO
God and his tenets when we are young. The bible has
many instructions that guide us through life. If we
only find God after we have blundered through most
of our adulthood, we miss the opportunity to live fully
in his grace and power. Children are not too young to
understand the basic principles that are outlined in God's
word; actually, God advises adults to be child-like in their
acceptance and embrace of his commands. Jesus said, "I
tell you the truth, unless you change and become like little
children, you will never enter the kingdom of heaven."
(Matt. 18:3) In fact, it is the duty of adults to introduce
Christ into the lives of their children. But it is never too
late; if you find him in your youth, or whenever you find
him – you have found the greatest treasure there is.

Let the little children come to me, and do not hinder them for the kingdom
of heaven belongs to such as these.

MATTHEWS 19:11

ABOUT THE AUTHOR

Toni Kendrick is a Christian woman with a strong commitment to living a full life shaped by the tenets of the bible. Born and raised in Chicago, now living in Charlotte, North Carolina and married for over 40 years, Toni believes her life's journey is stronger, more meaningful, and joyous because she recalibrates her contemporary values and routines with the doctrines set down in the bible. This practice has given her a life of unimaginable grace.